ANIMAL ALBUMS
THE BIRD FAMILY
BY ALEX MONROE
eureka!
EUREKA!, AN IMPRINT OF BELLWETHER MEDIA BY FLUTTERBEE

***Eureka!*** books turn real stories into unforgettable experiences. Clear, direct language and sharp, captivating imagery make it easy to follow your curiosity, one fascinating fact at a time.
Your Eureka! moment awaits!

This edition first published in 2026 by Bellwether Media, Inc.



For information regarding permission, write to Bellwether Media, Inc., Attention: Permissions Department, 3500 American Blvd W, Suite 150, Bloomington, MN 55431.

Library of Congress Cataloging-in-Publication Data is available at www.loc.gov or upon request from the publisher.

ISBN: 9798893048544 (hardcover)
ISBN: 9798893049541 (ebook)

Editor: Rebecca Sabelko Series Designer: Jeff Kollock

Printed in the United States of America, North Mankato, MN.

# TABLE OF CONTENTS


WHAT ARE BIRDS? 4
THE HISTORY OF BIRDS 6
LIFE CYCLE 8
BIRD LANGUAGE AND BEHAVIOR 10
BIRD FAMILY TREE 12
BIRD BIOGRAPHIES 14
BIRDS AND PEOPLE 42
GLOSSARY 46
WRITE ABOUT IT! 47
INDEX 48

# WHAT ARE BIRDS?

Birds are animals that are members of the *Aves* class. There are more than 11,000 species of birds. Birds live on every continent on Earth. They are found in nearly every habitat.

KINGFISHER

▲ BALTIMORE ORIOLE

▲ OSTRICH

## TAXONOMY CHART

Birds are incredibly diverse! They vary greatly in size, appearance, and behaviors. But they share several important features. All birds are warm-blooded and have backbones. They have feathers and wings. Their bills have evolved to be important tools. Most birds can fly and have hollow bones.

▲ TURQUOISE-BROWED MOTMOT

NORTHERN CARDINAL ▶

**CANADA GEESE ▲**
**autumn migration**

# THE HISTORY OF BIRDS

Birds evolved from small theropod dinosaurs around 160 million years ago. Most of these birdlike dinosaurs had feathers and wishbones. They had teeth and long, bony tails. Scientists suggest the first birds lived around 100 million to 85 million years ago. They looked different from modern birds. But they shared the features of all birds.

**DEINONYCHUS FOSSIL**
a theropod that had birdlike traits

## WONDERCHICKEN

**The first modern-looking bird is believed to be the wonderchicken. It lived around 66.7 million years ago.**

PEACOCK ▶

◀ LANNER FALCON

Birds evolved slowly. Hairlike feathers changed to become suited for flight. The animals' arms grew longer to form wings. Their chest muscles became bigger for flying. Their long, bony tails were replaced by fanned feathers. These adaptations helped birds become diverse.

# EVOLUTIONARY EXCELLENCE

**BEAK**
helps with eating, communicating, defense, and more

**LONG, FEATHERED WINGS**
allow for flight

**WIDE, MUSCLED CHEST**
powers flight

**HOLLOW BONES**
make body lightweight for flight

# LIFE CYCLE

**PARADISE TANAGER**
bright plumage

For many species, males attract females to mate. Some may deliver food to females or sing and dance. Others display bright plumage. Mates sometimes build nests together. Nests vary greatly among species. They can vary from a scrape on the ground to a collection of natural materials such as grass and fur placed in a tree.

**GROUND SCRAPE NEST**

**KING PENGUIN ▼**
sitting on an egg

**▲ SUNBIRD**
feeding hatchlings in its nest

Females lay hard-shelled eggs in nests. Parents sit on the eggs to keep them warm. Hatchlings are featherless. Parents feed their young. Many birds learn to fly when they become fledglings. They often stay close to their parents as they learn to survive on their own.

▼**BLUEBIRD** parent feeding its fledgling

## HOW MANY YOUNG?

**AMERICAN ROBIN**

**4 HATCHLINGS**

**WOOD DUCK**

**11 HATCHLINGS**

**GREATER FLAMINGO**

**1 HATCHLING**

**BLUE-FOOTED BOOBY**

**2 HATCHLINGS**

# BIRD LANGUAGE AND BEHAVIOR

## COMMUNICATION

Many birds use songs to communicate. They use aggression calls when defending their young and competing for territories, mates, or food. Companion calls are short notes between mates or group members. These calls let other birds know where they are. Prey species use alarm notes to warn of predators. Hatchlings' begging calls tell parents they need food.

◀ MOLTING

# BEHAVIOR

Birds molt to replace worn or damaged feathers. Some molt to change their plumage for the seasons. Molting also allows them to grow stronger feathers as they get older. Many birds preen their feathers to keep them clean and in good shape for flying.

**GLOSSY IBIS ▲**
**preening its feathers**

## MORE BEHAVIORS

**Many bird species migrate to food and nesting sites each year. Flocking is common during migration. Staying in groups helps keep birds safe, find food, and mate.**

# BIRD FAMILY TREE

▲ **PIGEONS AND DOVES**
more than 350 species

Rock pigeons were domesticated more than 5,000 years ago.

**WOODPECKERS, TOUCANS, AND BARBETS** ▲
more than 230 species

The drumming sounds woodpeckers make on wood are most often related to communicating with other woodpeckers.

▲ **PARROTS AND COCKATOOS**
more than 400 species

▲ **SHOREBIRDS**
more than 380 species

**PERCHING BIRDS** ▲
more than 6,700 species

▲ **OWLS**
more than 240 species

Great gray owls must dive through snow to catch prey. They can break through packed snow that can support a human that weighs 176 pounds (80 kilograms).

# AVES

**LANDFOWL ▲**
more than 300 species

**WATERFOWL ▲**
more than 170 species

**▲ KINGFISHERS**
more than 100 species

Laughing kookaburras' loud calls have been used in movies to sound like groups of monkeys.

**▲ SWIFTS, TREESWIFTS, AND HUMMINGBIRDS**
more than 470 species

**▲ FALCONS AND CARACARAS**
around 65 species

**+ MORE THAN 240 OTHER BIRD FAMILIES**

# AMERICAN ROBINS

American robins are often described as America's favorite songbird. These birds sing loud, cheerful songs.

## WHERE DO THEY LIVE?

Robins are frequently spotted in backyards, woodlands, and grassy areas across North America. Northern populations commonly migrate to warmer climates for winter.

## DIET

Robins forage for fruit such as mulberries and cherries. They use their bills to dig for worms and other invertebrates. The birds often beat insects such as butterflies against the ground. They eat their prey once it stops moving.

## APPEARANCE

American robins have blackish heads with grayish-brown backs and wings. White outlines their dark eyes. Their beaks are yellow. They are easily spotted by their orange breasts.

## SPECIES PROFILE

### RUFOUS-COLLARED ROBIN

- **Range:** southern Mexico to El Salvador and Honduras
- **Known for:** Rufous-collared robins are close relatives to American robins. The two species have similar songs and appearances.

## SIZE COMPARISON

| 33IN (84 cm) | 7IN (17 cm) | 10IN (25 cm) |
|---|---|---|
| great gray owl | downy woodpecker | American robin |

# BLUE-FOOTED BOOBIES

Blue-footed boobies' webbed feet turn blue from the fish they eat. Males rock from side to side to show off their feet to females. Females may respond by copying the dance.

## APPEARANCE

These seabirds have long, pointed bills and light-colored eyes. Brown and white feathers cover their heads. Their backs and wings are brown. Their breasts are white.

## DIET

Blue-footed boobies spend a lot of time in water. They dive in groups for anchovies and other schooling fish.

## WHERE DO THEY LIVE?

These boobies are found along the Pacific coast from northern Mexico to Peru. They also live on islands, including the Galápagos.

### DEEP DIVE

Blue-footed boobies can dive deeper than other animals that have similar diets. Some dive deeper than 66 feet (20 meters) to catch prey. They can stay underwater for more than 30 seconds.

### SPECIES PROFILE

#### RED-FOOTED BOOBY

- **Range:** Caribbean Sea and parts of the Atlantic, Indian, and Pacific Oceans
- **Known for:** Red-footed boobies are the smallest of the six booby species. These strong fliers spend more time at sea than other booby species.

## SIZE COMPARISON

| 16IN (41 cm) | 33IN (84 cm) | 21IN (54 cm) |
|---|---|---|
| crab-plover | blue-footed booby | wood duck |

# LAUGHING KOOKABURRAS

Laughing kookaburras' loud calls begin and end with low chuckling sounds. They let out a screaming laughlike sound in the middle.

## APPEARANCE

These kookaburras have light-colored heads and breasts with darker markings. They have large, boat-shaped beaks. Light blue dots cover the tops of their brown wings.

## DIET

Laughing kookaburras watch for invertebrates from perches. They swoop toward prey, land next to it, then grab it with their beaks. They may also dig for prey or grab insects from the air.

## SIZE COMPARISON

| 35IN (89 cm) | 16.5IN (42 cm) | 14IN (36 cm) |
|---|---|---|
| scarlet macaw | laughing kookaburra | rock pigeon |

## SNAKE ATTACK

Laughing kookaburras may hunt snakes up to 3 feet (1 meter) long. They beat snakes on the ground or their perches, then swallow them headfirst. The birds may drop snakes from up high to stun them.

## SPECIES PROFILE

### SPANGLED KOOKABURRA

- **Range:** Papua New Guinea
- **Known for:** Spangled kookaburras make harsh barking and violent screaming calls. They are smaller than laughing kookaburras. They have bright blue wings.



## WHERE DO THEY LIVE?

These birds are found in woodlands throughout eastern Australia. They are also spotted in farmlands, cities, and wetlands.

# CALIFORNIA CONDORS

California condors are among the largest flying birds. They can soar more than 200 miles (322 kilometers) in one day.

## WHERE DO THEY LIVE?

California condors are found in parts of California, northwestern Mexico, and the Grand Canyon. They nest in mountains, cliffs, and large trees.

## VULNERABLE SPECIES

▼CRITICALLY ENDANGERED▼

THREATS

habitat loss

lead poisoning

eating trash

collisions with power lines

CONSERVATION EFFORTS ▼

reducing the use of lead-based hunting bullets

breeding programs

habitat conservation

## DIET

California condors use excellent eyesight to scavenge carrion. They can eat up to 3.5 pounds (1.6 kilograms) of food at one time.

## APPEARANCE

These birds' naked heads and necks are yellow to reddish orange. Pointed feathers circle their necks. Black feathers cover their bodies. White feathers form long triangles on the undersides of their wings.

## SIZE COMPARISON

53IN (134 cm)

California condor

25IN (64 cm)

gyrfalcon

10IN (25 cm)

American robin

# CRAB-PLOVERS

Crab-plovers dig about 5 feet (1.5 meters) into sand to lay one large egg. The sand is warm enough that the birds do not need to sit on the egg.

## DIET

These birds mostly eat crabs. They sit and wait for crabs to appear, or they walk slowly to find prey. They use their bills to stab and crush prey.

## SIZE COMPARISON

**49IN** (125 cm)

greater flamingo

**33IN** (84 cm)

blue-footed booby

**16IN** (41 cm)

crab-plover

## WHERE DO THEY LIVE?

Crab-plovers live along the coasts of the Indian Ocean. They form large colonies on sandy beaches and rocky shores to mate and nest.

## SPECIES PROFILE

### PIED AVOCET

**Range:** parts of Europe, Africa, and Asia

**Known for:** Pied avocets have similar coloring to crab-plovers. But they have long, thin bills that turn upward.

## APPEARANCE

Crab-plovers have mostly white feathers. Black feathers mark their backs and wings. They have strong, black bills. Their long legs are bluish gray.

# DOWNY WOODPECKERS

Downy woodpeckers are the smallest and most widespread woodpeckers in North America.

## WHERE DO THEY LIVE?

Downy woodpeckers live throughout much of the United States and Canada. They thrive in many habitats. They are commonly found in woodlands.

= Range

DOWNY WOODPECKER
Range in the Wild

### LONG TONGUES

Woodpeckers' long tongues can be up to one-third of their body length. They fit in the birds' small heads by wrapping around their skulls.

## DIET

These birds use their pointed bills to peck into wood. They have long, barbed tongues and sticky saliva that capture insects. They also eat fruit and seeds.

## SIZE COMPARISON

14IN (36 cm)

rock pigeon

7IN (17 cm)

downy woodpecker

3.5IN (9 cm)

ruby-throated hummingbird

## APPEARANCE

Downy woodpeckers are mostly covered in black-and-white feathers. Their heads have wide stripes with a red patch on the back. Their wings are black with white dots.

## SPECIES PROFILE

### PILEATED WOODPECKER

- **Range:** parts of the U.S. and southern Canada
- **Known for:** Pileated woodpeckers are one of the largest woodpecker species. They have bright red crests. Males have red markings that look like a mustache.

# GREAT GRAY OWLS

Great gray owls use advanced hearing to find prey. Their left ear sits higher than their right ear. This allows them to pinpoint their prey.

## WHERE DO THEY LIVE?

These owls live in subarctic evergreen forests around the world. They perch at forest edges near open meadows.

## DIET

Great gray owls are specialized rodent hunters. They listen for prey from perches. Then they silently swoop toward prey and grasp it with their talons.

## SIZE COMPARISON

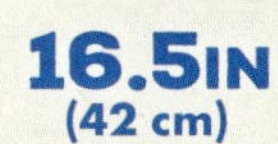

**33IN** (84 cm)

great gray owl

**16.5IN** (42 cm)

laughing kookaburra

**21IN** (54 cm)

wood duck

# APPEARANCE

Great gray owls have large, round faces. Their eyes and beaks are bright yellow. They have mostly gray feathers streaked with white and brown. Their white neck feathers look like a bow tie.

## SPECIES PROFILE

### GREAT HORNED OWL

- **Range:** throughout North America and parts of South America

- **Known for:** Great horned owls are named for the tufts of feathers on their heads. These owls are adapted to live well in nearly any climate.

## RODENT COUNT

Great gray owls can eat up to seven rodents per day in winter.

# GREATER FLAMINGOS

Greater flamingos help their ecosystems. Their poop and feeding methods improve water health.

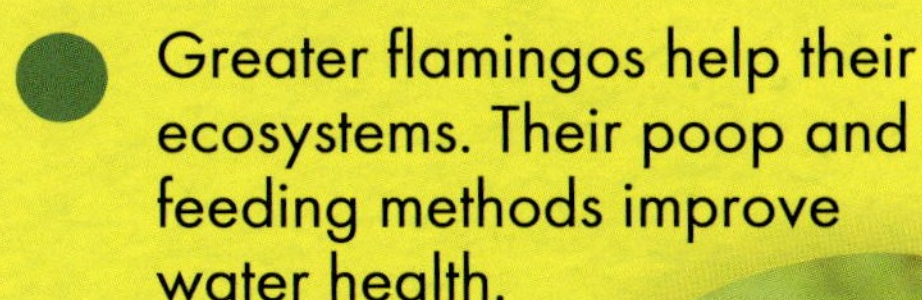

## APPEARANCE

These birds have small heads with black-tipped bills that are long and curved. Their pale pink feathers come from the pink shrimp they eat. Their necks and legs are long and thin.

## DIET

Greater flamingos eat invertebrates, microalgae, and seeds. With their heads upside down, they bury their open bills underwater. Comblike plates trap food as their tongues pump water in and out of their mouths.

# WHERE DO THEY LIVE?

Greater flamingos live in Africa, southern Europe, and western Asia. They prefer shallow coastal waters, wetlands, and rice fields.

= Range

### KNEE OR ANKLE?

**Many people think flamingos' knees bend backward. The visible joints are their ankles. Their knees bend forward. They are hidden under their feathers.**

## SIZE COMPARISON

**49IN** (125 cm)

greater flamingo

blue-footed booby

**16IN** (41 cm)

crab-plover

## SPECIES PROFILE

### AMERICAN FLAMINGO

- **Range:** coasts of the Caribbean Sea, northern coasts of South America, and the Galápagos Islands
- **Known for:** American flamingos were once considered the same species as greater flamingos. But American flamingos are smaller and have a darker color than greater flamingos.

# GYRFALCONS

Gyrfalcons are the largest falcons. Because they live in cold climates, scientists watch their behaviors to understand climate change.

▲ ROCK PTARMIGAN

## DIET

These powerful predators mostly hunt ptarmigan. They may strike prey from the air. Gyrfalcons also chase prey until it is tired. Then they use their sharp beaks and talons to finish the animal.

## FUTURE THREAT

▼ LEAST CONCERN ▼

THREAT

climate change

IMPACT ▼

changes in diet and breeding

habitat loss

increased human activity

extreme weather

## WHERE DO THEY LIVE?

Gyrfalcons live near water sources in arctic and subarctic habitats of North America, Europe, and Asia.

## SIZE COMPARISON

| 35IN (89 cm) | 27.5IN (70 cm) | 25IN (64 cm) |
|---|---|---|
| scarlet macaw | ring-necked pheasant | gyrfalcon |

## APPEARANCE

Many gyrfalcons have white feathers with black spots. Gray and dark brown feathers are also common. These birds have pointed wings and long tails. Females are much larger than males.

### SPEED DIVING

**Gyrfalcons can reach speeds up to 130 miles (209 kilometers) per hour while diving through the air.**

RING-NECKED
# PHEASANTS

Ring-necked pheasants are popular game for U.S. hunters. Males are known for their colorful plumage that includes shiny gold and copper.

## WHERE DO THEY LIVE?

These birds live throughout the northern hemisphere and parts of the southern hemisphere. They are found in farm fields, grasslands, and wooded areas.

## DIET

Ring-necked pheasants forage at dawn and dusk. They use their bills to dig for seeds, leaves, fruits, nuts, and insects. They scratch the ground for roots.

### INFREQUENT FLIERS

**Ring-necked pheasants do not fly often. But they can fly nearly 40 miles (64 kilometers) per hour to escape danger.**

## SIZE COMPARISON

**27.5IN** (70 cm) ring-necked pheasant

**14IN** (36 cm) rock pigeon

**3.5IN** (9 cm) ruby-throated hummingbird

MALES FIGHTING during mating season

SPECIES PROFILE

WILD TURKEY

Range:
North America

Known for:
Wild turkeys are commonly hunted in the U.S. They have shiny bronze and green feathers. Males are known for their showy tail fans.

## APPEARANCE

These birds are built like chickens. But they have long, pointed tail feathers. Males have bright red faces and shiny green necks with a white ring. Females have mostly brown feathers that lack shine.

# ROCK PIGEONS

Rock pigeons have been pets, food, and messengers for humans for thousands of years.

## APPEARANCE

Rock pigeons' feathers vary in color depending on where they live. But most are bluish gray. Shiny feathers cover their necks. Black markings cover their wings.

## FAMOUS PIGEON

### CHER AMI

- **Date:** **October 1918, World War I**

- **Famous for:** **Cher Ami flew 25 miles (40 kilometers) while injured to deliver an important message. His delivery saved nearly 200 American soldiers.**

## DIET

Rock pigeons mostly forage for seeds and fruits. Those that live in cities eat food scraps and food from bird feeders.

### FLYING HOME

**Rock pigeons were important messengers throughout history. They sent important messages during both World Wars. The messages helped save lives.**

## SIZE COMPARISON

| 33IN (84 cm) | 14IN (36 cm) | 16.5IN (42 cm) |
|---|---|---|
|  |  |  |
| great gray owl | rock pigeon | laughing kookaburra |

## WHERE DO THEY LIVE?

Rock pigeons have been introduced to nearly every continent. These birds are a common sight in large cities. Farmlands and rocky areas are their preferred mating sites.

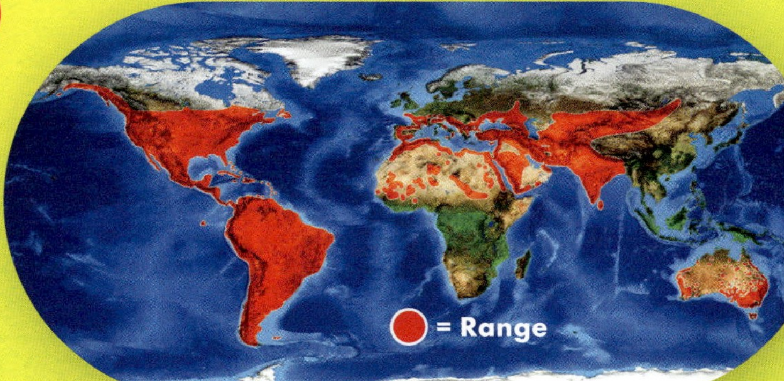

**ROCK PIGEON**
Range in the Wild

# RUBY-THROATED HUMMINGBIRDS

Some ruby-throated hummingbirds make great migrations each year. They can fly more than 500 miles (805 kilometers) nonstop.

## WHERE DO THEY LIVE?

Ruby-throated hummingbirds are found in southern Canada and the eastern U.S. They winter in southern Mexico and Central America. They prefer woodlands and gardens.

## DIET

Ruby-throated hummingbirds mostly eat flower nectar. They are most attracted to red and orange flowers. Their rapid wing flapping allows them to hover while they feed.

### FANCY FLIERS

Ruby-throated hummingbirds are fast flyers that can stop instantly. They can fly forward, up, down, or backward.

## SIZE COMPARISON

35IN (89 cm)
scarlet macaw

10IN (25 cm)
American robin

3.5IN (9 cm)
ruby-throated hummingbird

## SPECIES PROFILE

### ANNA'S HUMMINGBIRD

- **Range:** western North America
- **Known for:** Male Anna's hummingbirds fly up to 130 feet (39.6 meters) before they swoop toward mates. The display ends with a chirp sound made from their tails.

FEMALE

## APPEARANCE

These small hummingbirds have long, thin beaks and short wings. Shiny green feathers line their heads and backs. Males have bright red throats.

YOUNG MALE

# SCARLET MACAWS

Scarlet macaws live in pairs or family groups. They make loud, deep calls that carry long distances through forests.

## DIET

These birds eat nuts, seeds, fruits, and leaves. Their strong, curved bills allow them to easily break open nuts and seeds.

## FUTURE THREAT

▼ LEAST CONCERN ▼

▲ DEFORESTATION

**THREATS**

habitat loss from deforestation

pet trade

**IMPACT ▼**

extinct in parts of their original range

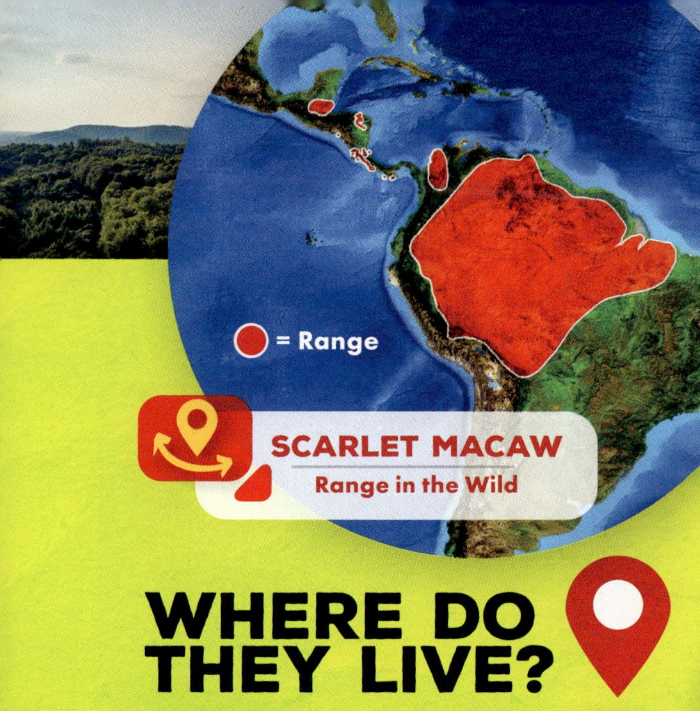


## WHERE DO THEY LIVE?

Scarlet macaws are found in tropical evergreen forests throughout Central and South America. They also live in wooded areas of savannas.

## SIZE COMPARISON

**35IN** (89 cm)

scarlet macaw

**49IN** (125 cm)

greater flamingo

**16.5IN** (42 cm)

laughing kookaburra

## APPEARANCE

Scarlet macaws have mostly bright red feathers. Their wings feature feathers that are blue and yellow with green tips. Their long, pointed tails make up half their body weight.

# WOOD DUCKS

Wood ducks nest in holes in trees. They easily fly through wooded areas. They often perch in trees.

## APPEARANCE

Wood ducks are recognized by their head crests. Males' crests feature shiny green feathers. Their red eyes and white necks are striking. Their breasts are reddish brown. Females are grayish brown with white patches around their eyes.

## DIET

These ducks forage for seeds, fruit, and invertebrates. They often feed in groups at the surface of water. They may dip their heads into shallow water to get food.

= Range

# WHERE DO THEY LIVE?

Wood ducks live in wetlands and forests near rivers and lakes throughout much of North America.

## SIZE COMPARISON

**53IN** (134 cm)

California condor

**21IN** (54 cm)

wood duck

**7IN** (17 cm)

downy woodpecker

## MANDARIN DUCK

- **Range:** parts of East Asia
- **Known for:** Mandarin ducks are close relatives to wood ducks. Both males and females have head crests. Males feature flashy feathers on much of their bodies.

# BIRDS AND PEOPLE

Birds have been important to humans for thousands of years. They are powerful symbols in many cultures. Chickens and other domesticated species are a major food source around the world. Many people hunt different kinds of birds for sport. Scientists often look to birds to understand the health of ecosystems.

CHICKEN FARM

FOWL HUNTING

Some of the ways people use birds can be harmful. The pet bird trade disrupts wild habitats. Many captured birds suffer from injuries and stress. Some species have gone extinct in their original ranges due to the pet trade.

## FOLKLORE PROFILE

**NAME:**

FENGHUANG

**COUNTRY:**

CHINA

**FAMOUS FOR:**

Fenghuang is a mythical bird. It has the head of a golden pheasant, the body of a Mandarin duck, the tail of a peacock, the legs of a crane, and the beak of a parrot. It is a symbol of peace and good fortune.

Birds are greatly impacted by human activities. Their habitats are destroyed by pollution and pesticides. People destroy woodlands for farming and development. Climate change is also changing habitats and disrupting migrations. Birds often fly into buildings and other structures.

Many organizations and governments work to repair and prevent further damage. Wildlife services fight to protect natural resources and habitats. Tools such as bird monitoring apps allow anyone to document sightings. People can help birds by keeping pet cats indoors, recycling, and reducing their energy use. Everyone can work to make the future bright for birds!

▲ **FIELD RESEARCH**
for tracking native birds

# GLOSSARY

**adaptations**—changes in animals over time that make them better able to hunt and survive

**aggression**—a readiness to fight

**barbed**—having sharp points that stick out

**carrion**—the rotting meat of a dead animal

**climate change**—a human-caused process in which Earth's average weather changes over a long period of time

**cultures**—the beliefs, arts, and ways of life in a place or society

**diverse**—made up of animals that are different from one another

**domesticated**—related to birds living near or around human settlements

**ecosystems**—communities of plants and animals that live in certain places

**evolved**—changed from one form into a new form

**extinct**—no longer living

**fledglings**—young birds that have feathers for flight

**forage**—to search for food

**habitat**—the natural home of plants and animals

**hatchlings**—baby birds

**hemisphere**—a half of the earth

**invertebrates**—animals without backbones

**microalgae**—aquatic plantlike organisms that cannot be seen by the naked eye

**migrate**—to move from one place to another

**molt**—to lose feathers in order to make room for new ones

**pesticides**—materials that kill pests such as insects or weeds

**plumage**—the feathers of birds

**pollution**—substances that make the earth dirty or unsafe; pollution usually comes from humans' actions.

**preen**—to use the bill to clean feathers

**saliva**—a watery fluid in the mouth

**scavenge**—to feed on carrion

**species**—groups of living things that are alike and can reproduce with one another

**talons**—sharp claws on birds that allow them to grab and tear into their food

**theropod**—a meat-eater dinosaur, such as a tyrannosaur or a velociraptor, that walked on two feet

**tropical**—related to the tropics where temperatures may be high

## WRITE ABOUT IT!

- What species of bird would you like to learn more about? **Why?**
- What bird behavior do you think is the most interesting? **Why?**
- **What** changes can you make in your life that could help keep birds and their habitats safe?

ALSO CHECK OUT

# INDEX


American robins, 9, 12, 14–15
blue-footed boobies, 9, 16–17
California condors, 20–21
Cher Ami, 34
crab-plovers, 12, 22–23
downy woodpeckers, 12, 24–25
evolutionary excellence, 7
Fenghuang, 43
great gray owls, 12, 26–27
greater flamingos, 9, 28–29
gyrfalcons, 13, 30–31
laughing kookaburras, 13, 18–19
ring-necked pheasants, 13, 32–33
rock pigeons, 12, 34–35
ruby-throated hummingbirds, 13, 36–37
scarlet macaws, 12, 38–39
species profile, 15, 17, 19, 23, 25, 27, 29, 33, 37, 41
taxonomy chart, 5
vulnerable species, 20, 30, 38, 43
wood ducks, 9, 13, 40–41





The images in this book are reproduced through the courtesy of: JAY, front cover (hummingbird), p. 1 (hummingbird); Paul, front cover (penguin), pp. 1 (penguin), 13 (waterfowl), 40 (top); Laura, front cover (flamingo), p. 1 (flamingo); Adrian Eugen Ciobaniuc, front cover (macaw), p. 1 (macaw); Eric Isselee, front cover (owl), pp. 1 (owl), 18 (main); Vitamirus, p. 3 (inset); Jim, p. 3 (roadrunner); bridgephotography, p. 4 (kingfisher); Miroslav Srb, p. 4 (oriole); sergei_fish13, p. 4 (ostrich); Dennis Donohue, p. 5 (geese); phototrip.cz, pp. 5 (motmot), 12 (shorebirds); Janet, p. 5 (cardinal); Daderot/ Wikimedia Commons, p. 6 (Deinonychus); Daniel J. Field/ Wikimedia Commons, p. 6 (fun fact); Leny Silina Helmig, p. 6 (peacock); EcoPrint, p. 6 (falcon); Lena, p. 7 (eagle); Luciano, p. 7 (hummingbird); ARSALAN, p. 7 (hawk); Wim, p. 8 (tanager); Kimpin, p. 8 (sunbird); ThirdeyeAvisionStudio, p. 8 (scrape); Roger, p. 8 (penguin); Melissa Burovac, p. 9 (bluebird); Josee Normandeau, p. 9 (robin); Cami Johnson, p. 9 (duck); mzphoto11, p. 9 (flamingo); MODpix, p. 9 (booby); RMMPPhotography, p. 10 (owl); cat on route, p. 10 (seagull); Svyatoslav Balan, p. 10 (nestlings); Elle777, p. 11 (molting); Man_IR, p. 11 (top middle); David Katz, p. 11 (penguin); Gordon, p. 11 (ibis); Albert Beukhof, p. 11 (fun fact); Joe Ravi, p. 12 (pigeons); Riverwalker, p. 12 (woodpeckers); ondrejprosicky, pp. 12 (parrots), 26 (top); dmnkandsk, p. 12 (perching birds); Stanislav Duben, p. 12 (owls); Piotr Krzeslak, p. 13 (landfowl); Michelle, p. 13 (kingfishers); Stan, pp. 13 (hummingbirds), 40 (bottom left); slowmotiongli, p. 13 (falcons); Gary, p. 14 (top); Aline, p. 14 (left); nd700, p. 14 (right); Bo, p. 15 (top); mdfazal, p. 15 (main); AGAMI Photo Agency/ Alamy Stock Photo, p. 15 (profile); Leon, p. 16 (main); MindStorm, p. 16 (left); Suzanne, p. 16 (right); Vaclav, p. 17 (left); Danita Delimont, pp. 17 (middle), 41 (left); JDMedia223, p. 17 (profile); Maridav, p. 17 (bottom); Kris, p. 18 (left); Audra, p. 18 (top); Ken Griffiths, p. 19 (left); Duncan Noakes, p. 19 (right); Wirestock, Inc./ Alamy Stock Photo, p. 19 (profile); jay, p. 20 (top); Sergii Figurnyi, p. 20 (left); PixilRay, p. 20 (right); photobyjimshane, p. 21 (top left); Josh, p. 21 (top right); Andy Dean Photography, p. 21 (main); FRAYN, p. 21 (middle); Red ivory, p. 22 (left); SIBU NOSTALGIA 2, p. 22 (middle); Dr Ajay Kumar Singh, p. 22 (top); prasanthdaskkm, p. 22 (main); Traveller MG, p. 23 (middle); aDam Wildlife, p. 23 (bottom); W. de Vries, p. 23 (profile); Mark, p. 24 (top); Steve Byland, pp. 24 (main), 25 (middle), 31 (right); Melinda Fawver, p. 25 (insect); Matt Cuda, pp. 25 (top), 36 (top); donaldluo, p. 25 (profile); Robert McAlpine, p. 25 (bottom); Hummingbird Art, p. 26 (middle); imaton, pp. 26 (bottom), 27 (bottom); David Davis, pp. 27 (profile), 43 (right); FotoRequest, p. 27 (main); Petr Šimon, p. 27 (fun fact); richardseeley, p. 28 (top); Martin and Dawn Q, p. 28 (bottom); rebius, p. 28 (main); Sourabh, p. 29 (top); Inichetti, p. 29 (middle); mrallen, p. 29 (profile); Col Armo/ Wirestock Creators, pp. 30 (top left), 42 (eagle); Ondrej Prosicky, p. 30 (top right); Mats, p. 30 (middle); Andrei Stepanov, p. 30 (bottom left, bottom right); Teresa, p. 31 (main); Bernie Duhamel, p. 32 (top); afefelov68, p. 32 (middle); WildMedia, p. 32 (bottom); Menno Schaefer, p. 33 (top); ManoStudioArt, pp. 33 (main), 37 (main); tomreichner, p. 33 (profile); Oggepogge/ Wirestock, p. 33 (right); War Department. U.S. Signal Corps/ National Museum of American History, p. 34 (profile); robert lee 1, p. 34 (main); Nuwat, p. 34 (top); Imago History Collection/ Alamy Stock Photo, p. 35 (fun fact); Katt Bee, p. 35 (middle); NA, p. 35 (top); Mike, p. 36 (bottom left); Phil, p. 36 (bottom right); fluffandshutter, p. 37 (profile); Agnieszka, p. 37 (middle); Deborah Ferrin, p. 37 (bottom); Karlos Lomsky, p. 38 (top left); petrsalinger, p. 38 (top right); Jakub, p. 38 (middle); Matyas Rehak, p. 38 (deforestation); Sam, p. 38 (bottom right); prin79, p. 38 (top); Sanit Fuangnakhon, p. 38 (main); Lecia Michelle, p. 40 (middle); Wandering views, p. 40 (bottom right); Adrian, pp. 40 (main), 44 (penguin); Harry Collins, p. 41 (middle); henk Bogaard, p. 41 (profile); tearsze, p. 42 (chicken farm); LUGOSTOCK, p. 42 (hunting); Wirestock, p. 43 (left); insima, p. 43 (profile); Thisislove, p. 44 (pollution); Maxim Kukurund, p. 44 (deforestation); sulit. photos, p. 44 (bottom); soft_light, p. 45 (top); Aoy_Charin, p. 45 (middle); yod67, p. 45 (bottom left); Maximillian cabinet, p. 45 (bottom right).